PREHISTORIC MONSTERS

PREHISTORIC MONSTERS

TEXT BY KATE BRASCH

PHOTOGRAPHS BY JEAN~PHILIPPE VARIN

Salem House Publishers
Topsfield, Massachusetts

First published in the United States by
Salem House Publishers, 1987,
462 Boston Street, Topsfield, MA 01983

Library of Congress Catlog Card Number: 86-61473
ISBN: 0 88162 255 9

Photographs © 1985 by Jean-Philippe Varin

This book was designed and produced by
John Calmann & King Ltd, 71 Great Russell Street,
London WC1B 3BN

Filmset by Tradespools Ltd, England
Printed in Hong Kong by
Mandarin Offset International Ltd

Title-page: Triceratops (see pp. 58-9)

CONTENTS

No one has ever seen the monsters in this book, and no one ever will see them. They lived and died long before man came on the scene. Scientists say that the first dinosaurs lived about 200 million years ago. The very last dinosaurs probably lived 60 million years ago. So they survived for a span of about 140 million years. Men have lived on earth for only about 2 million years, maybe 4 million years at the outside.

Creatures that manage to survive 140 million years – which is many times as long as men have lived so far – must have been very successful in all the most important ways. That is, they must have been quite good at living: feeding, giving birth and rearing their young and escaping from their enemies.

In this book, Jean-Philippe Varin, the photographer, shows you the monsters in their world: in field and stream, feeding and resting and fighting and playing. Iguanodon, for instance, had a backbone 30 ft (10 m) long, with its head 16 ft (5 m) above the ground. To feed, it would sit up, supporting itself on its strong legs and big tail. It would rest its front legs on a tree and it would rip off the tops of trees with its horny beak and eat them. Or look at Diplodocus. If we thought Iguanodon was big, with a backbone 30 feet long, Diplodocus was even bigger, with a body 88 ft (27 m) long. It probably stayed a lot in the water, very likely to escape fiercer, meat-eating monsters. Diplodocus did not have claws, and could only defend itself, we think, with the end of its whiplike tail. But how do we know this, and why do people, when they talk about the monsters, nearly always say *probably* and *we think*?

How we know about the monsters is because people have found their fossilized bones, teeth, eggs and footprints.

Scientists write *probably*, and *we think*, because they are still finding out, and because, any day, what they have written may be shown to be wrong. In 1787, a large dinosaur bone was found in New Jersey, USA. In the 200 years since then, bones, eggs, footprints and marks left by their skins on mud turned to rock have been found. All these finds – amounting to thousands of bones – aroused great interest. People began to ask questions, and answers were found. With so many clues, you would think that now, 200 years later, scientists would know the answers to most questions. But the interesting thing is that, as new finds are still being made, scientists come up with new answers to the same questions.

The questions are:

> *What did the animals look like?*
> *Were they stupid?*
> *What did they feed on?*
> *How did they behave?*
> *What sort of world did they live in?*
> *Were they cold- or warm-blooded?*
> *Were they slow and clumsy?*
> *Why did they die out?*

The answers scientists give today to these questions are, in some cases, different from the answers they gave twenty or thirty years ago. This is because new dinosaur bones, and even unknown dinosaurs, are still being discovered.

In 1677 Robert Plot's book *The Natural History of Oxfordshire* was published. In it he describes 'a real bone now petrified (a fossil) . . . it must have belonged to some greater animal than either an ox or a horse'. He thought it might have been an elephant brought over by the Romans. In the end he decided that it must have come from a giant man.

For the next 145 years, fossil bones kept on turning up. Scientists consulted each other and tried to guess what kind of an animal the bones had belonged to. But no one realized that they had found the remains of giant creatures which were no longer on the earth.

In 1822, James Parkinson published a drawing of a huge tooth. He named the animal it came from Megalosaurus ('great reptile') and thought it came from a giant animal, perhaps 36 ft (12 m) long and 8 ft (2.5 m) high. In the same year, 1822, Mary Anne Mantell, an English doctor's wife, made an exciting discovery. Her husband was a keen fossil collector. He wrote a book for which his wife drew the pictures, called *Fossils of the South Downs*. One day, while Dr Mantell was visiting a patient in Cuckfield, Sussex, his wife went for a walk and noticed some fossilized teeth embedded in a pile of stones waiting to be used for mending the road. These fossil teeth were very large, dark brown and shiny. Dr Mantell later found more bones in the quarry from which the stones had come,

Tyrannosaurus Rex, one of the largest reptiles of the Cretaceous period (see pp. 60 – 61).

Overleaf: A baby Diplodocus, newly hatched from one of the gigantic eggs laid by these huge creatures (see pp. 25 – 27).

An Iguanodon browsing (see p. 29).

but the whole skeleton was never discovered. Because there was no complete skeleton, scientists were left guessing.

Dr Mantell was delighted. He thought the teeth belonged to some giant plant-eater, a mammal. However, the rock in which the fossils were found was Cretaceous rock (see diagram on page 64). At the time, Cretaceous rock was thought to be too old to contain any mammals. So Dr Mantell looked for further clues, and decided that his fossil teeth were like those of an iguana lizard which lived – and still lives – in Central America. He called the animal Iguanodon ('iguana tooth') and, in 1825, he published a description of the animal as he thought it would have looked. He got it wrong – which is not surprising. One of his mistakes was to take the spiky bone that belonged in Iguanodon's thumb, and to draw it on top of its snout. Other scientists thought that the teeth might be fish teeth, or rhinoceros teeth.

From then on, in the 1830s, more giant bones were found, and scientists agreed that these were not mammals, but the bones of reptiles. By 1841, nine different sorts were known, and at a meeting of the British Association for the Advancement of Science, it was decided that the monsters should be called *Dinosauria*, the 'terrible lizards'.

Everyone was fascinated, and not only the scientists.

Men of science tried their hand at reconstruction and there were some interesting models made. The best ones were built of cement, stone and iron by a sculptor, and set in the grounds of Crystal Palace at Sydenham, London. There was a party for the monsters, and twelve of the guests had dinner *inside* the model of the Iguanodon. The only trouble was that – as we now know – all the models were wrong.

A great many dinosaur bones were found in the second half of the nineteenth century. A large number of these finds were in North America. But the real breakthrough came in Europe, in 1877. In a Belgian coalmine at Bernissat, miners were tunnelling at more than 1000 ft (300 m) below ground, when they realized that their tunnel was running through a mass of skeletons. These were identified as Iguanodons. It took three years to get them all out. Thirty-one of the Iguanodons are now in a Brussels museum, eleven of them mounted in a proper standing position. For the very first time, people could see a complete skeleton of a monster, and scientists could make serious and fairly accurate guesses at the muscles and skin which the creatures would have had.

At almost the same time, in the American West – in Colorado, Utah, Wyoming, Montana and New Mexico – Americans were discovering their own dinosaurs. One of the most exciting places was the area around the town of Medicine Bow, in Wyoming. Lying on the very surface of the ground were the bones of giant dinosaurs, in good condition. Scientists collected large numbers of nearly complete skeletons.

In one part of Colorado, so many finds were made that the local town, called Artesia, was renamed Dinosaur. Near there, an earth-movement had tilted strata (levels) that were full of dinosaurs' bones, so that the rock ended up as a cliff, 28 ft (9 m) high and 200 ft (60 m) long. If you go there, you could even now watch technicians freeing the bones from the cliff face.

But how did the bones get there? And how were they fossilized?

A time-explorer, transported back, say, 100 million years, would be the only man on earth. He would also not recognize much of the scenery around him. The continents and the seas at that time were shaped differently from the way we see them on the modern maps. The only animals he would recognize would be turtles, lizards and crocodiles. But he would also recognize, and be very frightened by, dinosaurs, whose fossil bones he would have seen in museums, and in books like this one.

Dinosaurs were fossilized this way.

Most of them lived on land, although they would venture into the water of rivers and swamps now and then. When a dinosaur died on land, other animals would eat the carcass and scatter the bones, or eat them. There would not be much chance of bones surviving. But if an animal died in the water, there was a better chance of the bones becoming fossils. The animal would sink to the bottom of the river or lake, and sand and sediment would cover its body. In time, layer upon layer settled on the bones. The weight of these wet layers, and the contact with the water and mineral salts, petrified and mineralized the bones. The rock mass above the skeleton might squash it and alter its shape a little, but there it would lie, now made out of stone instead of bone. But what has happened to the swampy world in which the dinosaurs lived and died?

As millions of years went by, there were changes in the earth's crust, some of them enormous changes. Part of the ocean might become a mountain range. A lake floor might become a plain. Cliffs crumbled. Rivers cut new valleys through the mountains. The landscape changed shape. Some fossils were no longer buried deeply. Some rose until they were almost under the skin of the earth's surface.

Men have always cut and dug the earth, but not very deeply. They have dug pits for clay, quarried for stone and made shafts and tunnels into the earth for coal. But the great discoveries of fossils were made in the second half of the nineteenth century, which was the first period of industrial development, when deep holes were dug for the foundations of buildings and bridges, and for railway tunnels.

And the fossil discoveries are not over. As you read this, workmen cutting tunnels, making freeways, excavating foundations for high-rise apartments or office blocks still discover monster fossils.

Soon after people made the first discoveries of dinosaurs, scientists began to notice that they formed groups depending on the shape of the animal's hip-bones. So dinosaurs are of two kinds: Lizard-hips (saurischia) and Bird-hips (ornithischia). Scientists think that both kinds probably developed from the same reptile ancestor.

Dinosaurs lived through three geological periods:

First, during the *Triassic* period (225 million years ago), there were lizard-hipped dinosaurs like *Plateo-*

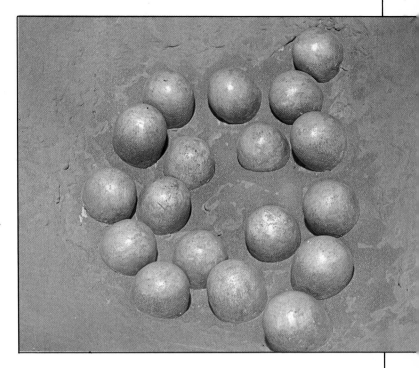

Protoceratops eggs. Protoceratops was a small Cretaceous dinosaur closely related to Triceratops (pp. 58 – 9). Its fossilized eggs and young have been found in the Gobi desert (Mongolia). These fossils proved that dinosaurs laid shelled eggs.

saurus and *Coelophysis*.

After the Triassic period came the *Jurassic* (190 million years ago). This is when the dinosaurs split into two kinds, the bird-hipped and the lizard-hipped. *Stegosaurus*, a dinosaur with bony plates sticking up like fins along its backbone, is an example of a 'bird-hip', while *Allosaurus* is an example of a 'lizard-hip'.

The Jurassic period gave way to the *Cretaceous* (65 million years ago).

The bird-hipped dinosaurs living then were of three kinds. There were armoured dinosaurs who relied on their armour to keep enemies off; the bird-footed beasts like *Corythosaurus*; and horned dinosaurs like *Triceratops*.

There were four main kinds of lizard-hipped dinosaurs living during the Cretaceous period: *Deinonycho-saurs* ('terrible claws'), fierce, pony-sized, meat-eating dinosaurs; *Coelurosaurs* ('lizards with hollows'), small, speedy, meat-eating dinosaurs with light skeletons; *Cannosaurs* ('flesh lizards')—these were the biggest of the meat-eaters; and *Sauropods* ('lizard-footed'): these were the biggest of them all.

At the end of the Cretaceous period – 70 million years ago – there were still plenty of dinosaurs. About

5 million years later, they had gone. We know that there were no dinosaurs living *after* the Cretaceous period because the strata of Cretaceous rock contain the fossils of many different dinosaurs. The first levels of rock *above* the Cretaceous levels contain a few fossils. And on the next level there are no dinosaur fossils at all.

People do not agree about the reason why the dinosaurs died out. Here are some of the arguments.

The climate changed at the end of the Cretaceous period and the continents altered their shape. Certain plants died – the plants on which the monsters fed – so it is possible that they simply starved. It is also possible that their bodies could not cope with the changes in climate. Birds and mammals can regulate their body temperature, but perhaps the dinosaurs could not do so. The dinosaurs had been used to a warm, even climate. Some scientists think that because dinosaurs were reptiles, they warmed up in the sun by day, and cooled down at night, like lizards. Others now think that certain kinds of dinosaurs were not cold-blooded like lizards, but warm-blooded in the way that we, and all mammals, are. Mammals produce heat by using muscles to burn up the food they eat.

Whether they were cold-blooded or warm-blooded, the change in climate meant trouble for the dinosaurs. Trees lost their leaves when winter came, and there was nothing for the herb-eaters to eat. As for the meat-eating ones, they fed off the herb-eating kind, so after a time, those dinosaurs had nothing to eat either.

There is not, so far, an answer to the question of why the dinosaurs died out, though there are lots of theories. There are, however, enough theories – more than sixty – to write a book about them!

A recent theory is that at the end of the Cretaceous period, a large asteroid, with a diameter of 4 – 9 miles (6 – 14 km), collided with the earth. This caused an enormous dust cloud, which blotted out the sun. Plants were destroyed and as a result the dinosaurs starved and died.

But it is possible that the dinosaurs simply died out naturally. In nature animals and plants come and go. Species develop, change, decrease and die out. Even the curator of the Fossil Amphibians, Reptiles and Birds at the Natural History Museum in London says that we do not know why dinosaurs died out.

How did dinosaurs live? The answer must be different for the three different periods (Triassic, Jurassic and Cretaceous) during which they flourished. Also, as some were the size of a whale and others no bigger than a sparrow, the answers will vary.

Starting with the Triassic period, the world was divided into two huge continents. Gondwanaland occupied the southern hemisphere and a northern continent covered what is now North America, the Atlantic Ocean, Europe, Great Britain and Russia. The continents were mostly desert and plains with sand and salty pools. But there were areas through which rivers ran and which had streams of fresh water. Here there were plants like ferns, and rushes grew in the water. The forests of pine trees might grow 200 ft (60 m) high. The temperature was warm all the year round. Scientists think that the plant-eating dinosaurs lived in small herds. They would warm up in the sun but then kept in the shade of the trees, sitting up on their hind legs and tails, munching plants. But the meat-eaters must have moved faster, to catch their prey. Large meat-eaters could use their weight to attack their prey. Others had horns, or claws or sharp teeth. Small ones could attack a plant-eating dinosaur far larger than themselves and tear it to bits.

The Jurassic period brought changes. Coloured fruits began to appear, there were blossoms and a kind of flower. A host of insects, reptiles and mammals appeared. New species also appeared among the dinosaurs, such as the armoured type.

When people talk about dinosaurs, they assume that they were slow and stupid. What did they think about, these dinosaurs? Were they really stupid?

Scientists have studied the heads of dinosaurs. The crocodile, a modern relative of the dinosaur, has a much smaller brain than there is space available in its skull. It is thought that dinosaurs' brains took up only half the space in the cavity. The size of the holes for eyes and ears show that they had eyes – sometimes very large – and ears to hear well. It is not likely that they could think. Instead, they reacted with their eyes, nose and ears to danger, to food, and to friends. Did dinosaurs have a voice? They probably had a powerful voice, again perhaps like that of the crocodile, which croaks to let other crocodiles know it is there, or barks when it is angry.

Some of the very big dinosaurs were certainly slow and ponderous. But the bird-footed dinosaurs, and all flesh-eating lizard-hipped dinosaurs, walked and ran on their long legs. The *Coelurosaurs* – the lizards with hollows – small, agile, flesh-eating dinosaurs with very light skeletons, could run fastest. They may have run as fast as 35 mph (55 kph).

How did dinosaurs reproduce? It is possible that some dinosaurs produced live young. Tiny complete dinosaurs have been found inside dinosaur skeletons. Were they born live, like mammals – or were some dinosaurs cannibals? Some dinosaurs certainly laid eggs. Eggs belonging to *Sauropods* (the very largest dinosaurs) have been found, as well as eggs belonging to *Ornithopods* – the bird-footed dinosaurs – and to armoured dinosaurs. The eggs vary from smaller than a hen's egg to ten times its size. The mother laid her eggs in a nest, a sort of large mud pie with a hollow in the middle. The largest find of eggs so far is of a nest holding 18 *Protoceratops* eggs (see picture on p. 11). The Protoceratops was 6 ft (2 m) long, with four strong legs and a frill at the back of its head.

There are still places in the world where you can find dinosaur bones. Dinosaur hunters have gone out to remote parts of the world to look at a new dinosaur find. They come back and write up what they have seen, so that a large expedition can be organized. This is when problems start. The old sites were in Europe and America. The new sites are in far-distant places, often in seldom-visited parts of countries which have become independent only recently. Two things are needed: very careful planning and a sponsor to pay for the expedition. The planning can take years. When an expedition has found dinosaur remains and brought the collection back to its own country, research begins. Nowadays when the research is finished, the remains are returned to the country where they were found. Naturally a country wants to keep its own dinosaurs.

In the 1980s there was a new problem. An expedition looking for dinosaurs in an African country ran into trouble with the authorities. The authorities wanted to know if the expedition had really come to hunt dinosaurs? Or were they looking for valuable minerals perhaps, to dig up, put into crates and take back to Europe? One expedition, in 1977/78, suddenly found itself in an African prison. After a lot of trouble, they were freed by the Military Governor.

What an expedition needs today is very different from what the nineteenth-century dinosaur hunters needed. In the 1980s, the members of an expedition to a remote area must take everything with them for the period they are in the field. As the new sites are often in the desert – bones keep well there – they must make sure they have enough water. The fossil-hunters will need four-wheel-drive cars for the rough ground, and lorries to transport the specimens; picks, shovels,

Volcanic eruptions were among the perils facing the dinosaurs.

hammers and chisels, as well as crates. They have to have plaster of paris, to make protective jackets for the dinosaur bones, so that they do not break on the way home. Once home, highly skilled technicians, using newly developed methods, measure and draw and make display models.

There have been exciting finds made by dinosaur expeditions this century. The Germans went to East Africa from 1909 to 1912. They brought back a lot of fossil dinosaur bones, the most exciting being a skeleton of *Brachiosaurus* for the Museum of Humboldt University, Berlin. In the 1920s the Americans sent expeditions to Central Asia. In the 1950s, the Russians sent dinosaur expeditions to Mongolia. In the late 1960s and early 1970s there were joint Polish-Mongolian expeditions to the Gobi Desert. And China has been collecting dinosaurs for the past 30 years. The largest known duck-billed dinosaur, *Shantungosaurus*, is in the Natural History Museum, Peking.

We would all like to go on a dinosaur-hunting expedition and find fossils. Meanwhile, here are 56 photographs of the monsters, as they moved through their territory, to help you imagine their lives, lost in the mists of more than 140 million years ago.

◁Previous page: **AMEBELODON** (Pliocene)
This was a long-jawed mastodont, also known as a shovel-tusker. It scooped up plants with the flattened tusks.

▽**ALLOSAURUS** (Jurassic – Cretaceous)
This carnivore grew to 30 ft (10 m) in length and could walk at a speed of 5 miles (8 km) an hour, that is, twice the speed of herbivorous dinosaurs. It lived off amphibian creatures like Brontosaurus, which it is devouring here. It was thought to hunt prey, since it had sharp teeth and claws as well as jaws with a powerful grip. But it is possible that it was simply a scavenger, feeding off carcasses killed by other animals. Allosaurus fossils have been found in Wyoming and in Colorado, in the western United States.

ANKYLOSAURUS (Cretaceous)   ▷
Ankylosaurus means 'stiff lizard'; the whole animal was covered in heavy armour. The name is somewhat misleading, for the thick, oval plates of bone of which the armour was made were articulated: the animal could move them independently. Ankylosaurus had a broad, heavy body and short, solid legs. Its tail was thick and powerful, and ended in a huge, bony club. The whole creature measured about 14 ft (4.5 m). With its only other defence its blunt, feeble teeth, Ankylosaurus would have had to crouch down if attacked. That way its legs and belly were protected. Ankylosaurus lived in North America, Central and South Asia and Central Europe.

◁ **ARSINOITHERIUM** (early Oligocene)

This is the skull of one of the first successful mammals. On top of its nose bones it carried two enormous sharp horns. But in spite of its fierce appearance, this creature lived on plants growing in damp forests and on the edge of swamps. Arsinoitherium's limbs were very heavy; it appears to have been a slow-moving animal more like a hippopotamus than a rhinoceros. It grew to a length of 10 ft (3 m), and seems to have been a specific African animal. It is named after the Egyptian princess Arsinoe, a daughter of Pharaoh Ptolemy I, who lived in the 3rd century BC.

▽ **BRONTOPS ROBUSTUS** (Oligocene)

Brontops, a mammal which belonged to the rhinoceros family and which could grow to a length of 15 ft (4.7 m), spread out from North America to Asia. Some of them appeared in Europe. Unusually, these animals became extinct during the middle of the Oligocene – for what reason is at present unknown.

◁ **CAMPTOSAURUS** (Upper Jurassic) ▷

A Camptosaurus measured anything from 5 to 16 ft (1.5 to 5 m), and was a herbivore, browsing like a cow in the meadows. With no armour or sharp claws, its only defence was to run for its life when attacked. Camptosaurus's posture was more upright than that of the meat-eating dinosaurs which attacked it. It probably stood upright to detect approaching enemies. The front end of its jaw ended in a beak. As it had no teeth in the front of the jaw, it may have used this beak to tweak off leaves and small twigs, which it chewed with the teeth in its cheeks.

▽ **BALUCHITERIUM** (Oligocene to early Miocene)

These mammals belonged to a branch of the rhinoceros family which developed amphibious habits and were a hornless variety. A Baluchiterium was a large animal with stocky limbs. Those found in Mongolia grew into giants, 18 ft (5.5 m) at the shoulders.

◁Previous page: **CORYTHOSAURUS** (Upper Cretaceous)

Our picture shows two giant Corythosaurus dinosaurs at sunset. They belong to the duckbill or Hadrosauridae family. The Corythosaurus was a large type, and is thought to have weighed 3.8 tons, with a length of about 30 ft (9 m). Its feet had toes, each of which ended in a small hoof. A domelike structure capped its skull.

▽**DIMETRODON** (Permian)

This curious-looking reptile carried on its back long spines which probably had skin stretched between them. The animal may have used this spiny crest as a fan to cool itself. From the teeth found, Dimetrodon is believed to have been a hunter of smaller reptiles and of amphibians. Its bones have been found in North America. It grew to a length of about 6 ft (2 m).

DIPLODOCUS (Jurassic)   ▷

This creature was one of the largest dinosaurs: it could reach nearly 88 ft (27 m) in length. At the end of its very long, curving neck was a ridiculously small head. Its jaws were not strong and it had teeth rather like pegs or spoons, so that it could eat only soft vegetation such as leaves or fruit. It had strong legs rather like an elephant's. The back legs were longer than the front ones. The tail was very long, thick and strong at the base, slender and whip-like towards the tip. It is possible that the tail was used as a defence weapon.

DIPLODOCUS

The skull of the Diplodocus, and, right, a view of the creature from behind showing its thick strong tail. There has been some discussion among scientists over whether this creature was amphibious, but it is generally believed that it did live in lakes and swamps, and was a powerful swimmer, as our pictures indicate.

▽ **ELASMOSAURUS** (Upper Cretaceous)

This was one of the largest reptiles, reaching a length of about 42 ft (13 m), of which 22 ft (7 m) were its neck. The head was quite small, and it had a dog-like snout with sharp teeth. But the most interesting thing about this creature was the immensely long, snake-like neck, made up of 76 bones. No other animal had, or has, such a large number of neck vertebrae. An Elasmosaurus would spot some creature such as a fish, or a flying lizard, while swimming. Then its coiled neck would shoot out very fast and seize its prey. In this picture it is fighting with a smaller reptile, a Tylosaurus. Some Elasmosaurus fossils have been found with part of the stomach content. Scientists have listed the contents as pebbles, as well as bits of fish, flying lizards and cuttle-fish. The pebbles were probably swallowed to help break up the food in the stomach.

IGUANODON (Jurassic – Cretaceous) ▷

The first remains of this animal – a row of teeth – were found in England in 1822, and gave it its name of 'iguana tooth', because the teeth resembled those of the iguana lizard of Central America. Since then many sections of skeletons have been found. Miners tunnelling underground in Belgium came across a great mass of them, and many more were found in the USA. The Iguanodon, which measured about 35 ft (11 m) from nose to tail, is perhaps the most commonly known prehistoric creature. With its long hind legs, long thick tail, and upright stance, it looked ferocious, but was in fact another herbivore, tearing off leaves from the tops of trees.

△ **MAMMUTHUS** (late Pleistocene)   ▷

Various kinds of mammoths developed during the Pleistocene period. One of them, the Columbian mammoth (right), was a large elephant with twisted tusks. It lived in the south-eastern part of North America, in what is now South Carolina, Georgia and Louisiana, roaming the warm steppes, or inhabiting river banks and deltas. Its height from shoulders to ground was 12 ft (3.7 m). Herds of mammoths would live in company with other herds of grazing animals, such as horses, bison, camels and steppe antelopes.

◁Top: **MEIOLANIA PLATICEPS** (Cretaceous)
The horned turtle was one of a variety of prehistoric turtles. Turtles basically like those living now were in existence during the Triassic, Jurassic and Cretaceous periods. Although its shell was like that of modern turtles, the creature could not retract its head or tail.

◁Bottom: **MEGALOCEROS** (late Pleistocene)
Megaloceros was a giant deer-like animal, about 6 ft (1.8 m) tall at the shoulder, with immense antlers. It was similar to the modern reindeer, and lived in the cold steppes and the tundra. Complete skeletons have been found in Ireland, preserved in peat.

△**MEGALOSAURUS** (Jurassic – early Cretaceous)
The Megalosaurs, 'big lizards', were large upright carnivores, with sharp, serrated teeth. The animal measured about 18 ft (6 m) in length, and standing up, 9 ft (3 m). It forelegs were strong and it had powerful hind legs. All four feet had three large claws. Footprints of these creatures, some making trackways, have been discovered in rocks in Southern England.

Megalosaurus's tail was large and muscular and was used for balance when walking. From one set of footprints scientists have worked out that a Megalosaurus once stalked a large plant-eating dinosaur, at about 5 miles (8 km) an hour.

◁ **MOA EURYAPTERIX** (Pleistocene to recent)

Moa is a Maori word, and was used quite recently by the people of New Zealand, where it lived, to describe a relative of the ostrich. Moa Euryapterix could not fly, but it did have very strong legs for running. Its height was about 7 ft (2.2 m). Its head was small and the beak was wide, curved and blunt. It lived in meadows and forests. Remains have been found in caves, where it probably sheltered. From stones found in its stomach it seems that the Moa was a vegetarian and swallowed the stones to grind its food.

▽ **MOROPUS** (Miocene)

This mammal looked like a cross between a horse, a bear and a camel, with long claws on the three toes of each foot instead of hoofs. It belonged to the clan of the chalicotheres, which are now extinct. Although Moropus looked rather like a horse, its front legs were longer than the back ones so that its back sloped, rather like the modern hyena.

Overleaf: **NOTHOSAURUS** (Jurassic) ▷

Nothosaurus was a marine amphibian, a powerful swimmer with its paddle-shaped front limbs. Remains have been found in what is now Central Europe, which would have been under the sea in the Jurassic period. Nothosaurus had a long, thin head, very long front teeth and smaller back teeth. It lived on a diet of fish which it was well equipped to catch, with its razor-sharp teeth and streamlined body. It was able to walk on land, so it was well adapted to life both in and out of the water. Nothosaurus could grow to a length of 10 ft (3 m).

PARASAUROLOPHUS (Upper Cretaceous)
The Parasaurolophus lived in North America and could grow to about 33 ft (10 m). It had a duckbill, and a crest. Its skin was covered with small scales, and its fingers and toes were webbed. But, unlike a duck, the Parasaurolophus had splendid teeth. Indeed, we know what it ate, for a fossil of the creature has been found complete with stomach contents. These included a mass of needles from a type of pine tree, as well as twigs, seeds and fruit.

△ **PAREIASAURUS** (Permian)

This giant reptile, 11 ft (3.5 m) in length, looked something like a rhinoceros, but without horns. Its limbs sprawled rather like those of a salamander. It used them like levers to raise itself off the ground. Pareiasaurus walked in a very primitive way because its limbs were angled at 90° instead of the normal angle at which other large animals' limbs are set. Because of this, Pareiasaurus needed very strong muscles to move its legs. Remains have been found in South Africa, Russia, Texas and New Mexico.

Overleaf: **PTERANODON** (late Cretaceous) ▷

Pteranodon was the largest of the prehistoric winged reptiles. Its fossilized bones have been found in the USA, in Kansas. Pteranodon means 'wings and no teeth'. Its skull was very long. The beak was probably used for catching fish, and the long crest at the back probably acted as a rudder, or may have been there just to balance the beak. Its body was about 9 ft (3 m) long. It had small legs, but its wingspan was 26 ft (8 m), which gave it a great mastery of air currents.

PLESIOSAURUS (Lower Jurassic)

Plesiosaurus means 'swan-lizard'. Some of these creatures had long, snaky necks. Their bodies were short and flat. The head was quite small in the long-necked kind, while on the short-necked Plesiosaurus the head was quite large. Our pictures show the long-necked form both underwater and on the surface. It was about 6 ft (2 m) long, and used its paddle-like legs and its pointed teeth to catch fish. It is thought that it could also rear up to catch flying animals. Pebbles have been found in the stomach of Plesiosaurus, which it had apparently swallowed to help break up the food.

POLACANTHUS (Cretaceous)
This is one of the armoured dinosaurs. Polacanthus had a double row of spikes running along its back and tail. Rows of overlapping small bones protected it in the hip region, like a bony blanket.

PLATEOSAURUS (late Triassic – early Jurassic) ▷
This enormous herbivore could grow to a length of 20 ft (6.5 m). It had a small head, long neck and long tail, and could rear up on its hind legs. Its name means 'flat lizard'.

▽**SCOLOSAURUS** (Permian)
Scolosaurus was a member of the Ankylosauridae, 'stiff lizards'. It was heavily armoured and measured about 20 ft (6 m).

▽**SMILODON** (Pleistocene)   ▷
This was the ancestor of the tiger – but bigger and heavier than the modern animal. With its sabre teeth and strong, heavy paws it could tear down even quite large prey, like the mammoth in the bigger picture.
                                               ▷
Overleaf: **STRUTHIOMIMUS** (Upper Cretaceous)
The ostrich dinosaur, Struthiomimus, was a very fast runner. Lightly built and about 10 ft (3 m) in height, it had three claws on both fore and back legs.

SYNTHETOCERAS (Pliocene)   ▷
These were deer-like ruminants. There were a variety of deer-like animals, the males having horns of all shapes and sizes, including a kind with six pairs of horns. Synthetoceras had horns over its eyes which were directed backwards, and on its nose it had a growth in the shape of a Y which was longer than its head.

Top right: **STYRACOSAURUS** (Upper Cretaceous)   ▷
The name means 'spike lizard'. The Styracosaurus had a frightening appearance, but it fed only on vegetation. On its nose there was a sharp horn, and it also carried six long pointed spikes on its head, probably for defence. Beneath the spikes, on either side of the head, was a frill of skin. Its whole body was protected with leathery skin, pieces of which have been found. It is thought that Styracosaurus roamed in great herds throughout western North America.

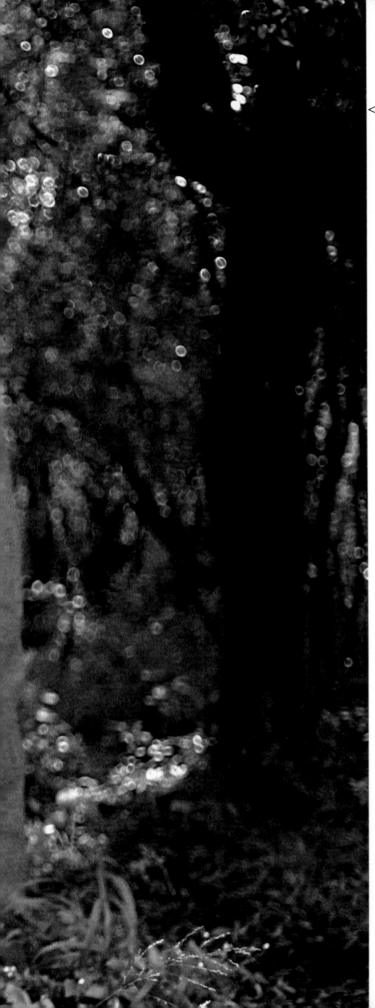

◁ STEGOSAURUS (Cretaceous)

Along the spine of Stegosaurus ran two rows of large, bony plates. Whether they were there to frighten predators or to protect is hard to decide. The protection theory does not really stand up as the flanks were unprotected. One idea put forward by a Finnish scientist is that Stegosaurus curled up like a hedgehog when attacked. Another theory is that the plates acted as heat exchangers, regulating the animal's temperature. The creature did not have many teeth: the front of the jaw was toothless. An interesting feature was the large lump on the spinal cord near the animal's hip. This was not a 'second brain' as some people have thought, but a glycogen gland, giving extra energy for the powerful back legs. Modern birds have such glands. Stegosaurus fossils have been found in Colorado, USA.

Overleaf left, centre: TRACHODON (Cretaceous) ▷

Trachodon (Anatosaurus) had a flat, low head and a snout like a duck's bill. It measured about 30 ft (9 m). Its back legs were thicker than the front ones; the front ones had webbing between the toes, so it could swim. Remains have been found near North American lakes and rivers. It was not a meat-eater, and fed off plants with the help of about 1000 tiny teeth which crowded its jaws.

Overleaf right: TELEOCERAS (Pliocene) ▷

This animal was the forerunner of the present rhinoceros. Its body was longer than that of the modern animal and its legs were shorter, so that the barrel-shaped body almost touched the ground. It seems that this animal lived in the water, and used its short limbs for swimming rather than walking. It grew to a length of about 13 ft (4 m), and its body was 3 ft (1 m) high.

TRICERATOPS (Late Cretaceous)

Triceratops, one of the heaviest horned dinosaurs, could grow to a length of 30 ft (9 m) and weighed $8\frac{1}{2}$ tons. This huge herbivorous creature carried two large horns, about 3 ft (1 m) long, which curved forwards and outwards, and a smaller one which was set on its nose. It had a bony neck frill, a massive body, a powerful short tail and legs like pillars, with hoofs. Triceratops lived, like the rhinos of today, near swamps and lakes, as well as on higher ground where there were trees such as gingkos, poplars, oaks and maples. Here Triceratops roamed singly or in small groups. It probably used its horns to fight rivals during the mating season. Triceratops fed on leaves and plants. In each jaw there were about 35 tightly packed columns of teeth, one below the other so that, as a tooth wore out, the one behind would come into use.

△ TYRANNOSAURUS REX (Upper Cretaceous)

◁ Tyrannosaurus Rex means 'king of the tyrant reptiles'. It grew to a length of nearly 50 ft (15 m) and weighed about 10 tons. Much detective work has gone into the reconstructions of this animal, as, so far, no complete skeleton has been found. Scientists now believe that Tyrannosaurus could not take large strides and moved very slowly, say, 3 miles (5 km) per hour, slower than the average person's walking speed. In spite of its terrifying appearance, therefore, Tyrannosaurus was not equipped to be a hunter. All it could do was to scavenge the remains of the meat other animals had killed. Its teeth, 6 in (16 cm) long and very slim, like blades, were probably too weak for attacking other reptiles. Its tiny forearms have puzzled scientists. Two small claws on its hands were probably stuck into the ground to help the creature get up, for otherwise its heavy body would have slid forward on the ground.

Overleaf: **UINTATHERIUM** (Middle Eocene) ▷
Uintatherium was one of the first successful mammals. It was about the size of a rhinoceros, and was related to the elephant. Its brain was very small. On its skull it carried three pairs of 'horns' covered with skin. It had two teeth sticking out from its jaw like curved sabres. In spite of its appearance Uintatherium was not a fierce flesh-eating creature. It used its sabre teeth to pick up plants growing in marshes, lakes and streams. The Uintatherium was found in western North America, and its habitat was waterside or marshland.

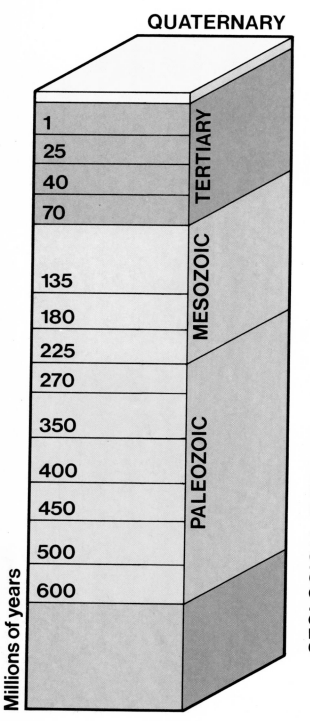

QUATERNARY

Millions of years

1	TERTIARY
25	
40	
70	
	MESOZOIC
135	
180	
225	
270	PALEOZOIC
350	
400	
450	
500	
600	

GEOLOGICAL SYSTEMS (maximum thickness in feet)

Pliocene

Miocene

Oligocene

Eocene

Cretaceous

Jurassic

Triassic

Permian

Carboniferous

Devonian

Silurian

Ordovician

Cambrian

Pre-Cambrian